ABC FEELINGS is an interactive book for adults and children to learn, share and experience feelings together. Through greater acceptance and understanding, communication is enhanced, leading to more meaningful relationships.

WHAT OTHERS ARE SAYING ABOUT ABC FEELINGS:

"I have recommended ABC Feelings to dozens of my clients and have seen it's effectiveness with their children as well as those of my family members."
– Phyllis R. Cazares, Ph.D., Clinical Psychologist

"Why wait for a crisis to implement these tools [ABC FEELINGS products]? Incorporate them across the curriculum — no matter the subject or age, integrate them into family life daily, as a part of everything!"
– Vicki Simms, Elementary School Teacher

"I think the book is good for children to learn about their feelings, even the parts about being sad, lonely and mad. Using it has helped me feel mature as I can understand my feelings."
– Amy Martinson, age 9

"Children need to understand what their own feelings mean -- anger, fear, pain, love, disgust and even boredom. ABC FEELINGS is a step in that direction. Once a child can put a label on a feeling, it is easier for him/her to understand it. Adults can get a better understanding of their child's non-verbal feelings by how he/she projects those feelings onto paper."
– Dr. Lendon Smith, Pediatrician, Renowned Lecturer and Author

"ABC FEELINGS has the ability to carefully reach within and bring forth a powerful energy longing to be shared – like the flower whose gentle strength and sure growth splits the stone."
– O. Fred Donaldson, Ed.D., Educational Consultant

"I see your book as an excellent reference on "feelings" for the creative teacher and parent. It is a unique concept to relate the alphabet with human emotions. The child will see inside himself, identify with his feelings and the adult will learn more about the child."
– Dr. Marcia Stillman, Doctor of Education

ABC Feelings

A Learning/Coloring Book

by
Alexandra
Delis-Abrams, Ph.D.

Illustrations/Book Design by
Shari Scott

Edited by
Joan Follendore

ABC FEELINGS, INC.
Formerly Adage Publications
P.O. Box 2377 • Coeur d'Alene, Idaho 83816-2377
e-mail: feelings@iea.com

Printed by Media Lithographics
Los Angeles, California
Second Printing, 1991 revised
Third & Fourth Printing, 1993
Fifth Printing, 1995 revised
Sixth Printing, 1997 revised
ISBN 1-879889-00-5

DEDICATION

My thanks go into the Universe for providing me the perfect input at the perfect moment, beginning with my loving husband, Gene; my three magnificent children — Jeffrey, Christopher and Danielle; Joanie, my encouraging editor; Jean, my perceptive publisher; Shari, my talented illustrator; Dona and Diane, two special friends; Dana, my supportive niece; Cami and Caroline, two first-grade teachers; many children from a local school who gave me their pure and inspiring honesty and wisdom; and last, but not least, Austin, a six year-old, sweet soul whose enthusiastic critique motivated me.

FOREWORD

My purpose in writing ABC FEELINGS was to create a tool for young children to become aware of, and understand, their feelings. It will also familiarize them with their ABCs, as a coloring/cognitive learning book with space for creative expression of twenty-six of your child's feelings.

When the seed of self-esteem is beginning to germinate, children can learn to recognize their many feelings. Feelings are wonderful! They make us feel alive. They're not necessarily good or bad . . . they just are. Feeling happy doesn't make us a good person, and feeling mad doesn't make us a bad person.

My three children were very young when my husband and I participated in a course on "Parent Effectiveness Training." I benefitted from it as an individual, aside from being a parent. I learned the significance of feelings and how they affect the quality of my life.

Through that awakening, I recognized our children have feelings that deserve respect also. It occurred to me that when children are learning their ABCs, they are most receptive to comprehending feelings and their influences.

Wanting to enter the healing profession, I was guided to the field of psychology. The study of "FEELINGS" attracted my interest when I saw that people suffer depression, stress, disease — a state of imbalance — when they fail to understand the source of their feelings.

An essential skill in the practice of psychology is truly listening. That skill proved innate in my former profession as an interviewer/recorder of life histories on tape — to preserve family legacies. This subtle, but effective, form of psychology demonstrated the need people have to understand the origin of their feelings. The insights revealed aroused the interviewees' suppressed emotions and gave them the awareness to accept and honor their feelings. Unexpressed emotions lingering from childhood are an underlying cause of maladies. This book helps both children and adults express those emotions and heal imbalance that result from their suppression.

INTRODUCTION

This book is designed for mutual sharing — so the child and the reader can practice being aware of their feelings. By discussing each ABC Feeling with the reader, the children don't stifle their feelings. They experience or feel the feelings, emotionally and physically. This process promotes self-acceptance which gives birth to inner peace and self-confidence.

The following "Reader's Guidelines" are simple, and using them will achieve the intended results:

1. Find an appropriate time to experience the ABC FEELINGS book with the child. Some may want to spend several minutes on each letter, and others may be anxious to move on to the next. Either way is fine. Whether you take a few minutes with one or two words, or an hour or more to cover the entire book, do so at a time when you are not rushed and/or the child is not tired.

2. Be open and honest while you share.

3. Listen, really listen, to what the child is saying, and be ready to interact with him/her, and explore the thoughts more deeply.

4. Judge not. Notice any desire you might have to judge, and instead — accept the child's sharing, allowing the feelings to be felt and expressed.

5. Allow your "inner child" to come out and play with the feelings you're discussing.

6. Keep in mind, this process is meant to be informative and enjoyable.

My niece, Dana, and her four-year-old son, P.J., read an early sample of this book. While they were discussing the letter "M" for "mad," she asked if he could think of a time when he felt mad. He told her about a time his friend hit him with a toy. They proceeded to discuss the emotions surrounding that particular incident, which gave her deeper insight of P.J. "What a great learning tool for me as a parent," Dana declared.

Each letter of the alphabet has five aspects: the large letter itself; a statement associated with the feeling beginning with that letter; the illustration depicting that feeling (which can be colored in by the child); suggested dialogue "ice breakers" for the reader and child; and a blank page opposite, for the child to draw an illustration of that feeling.

These special moments together will be remembered long after the child's ABCs have been mastered. The two of you are establishing models for communication, as the child matures. In doing so, a nurturing, close relationship is created, based on understanding, respect and love.

This blank page is for you to draw or write how you felt when you were feeling accepted.

A *is for feeling ACCEPTED*

"I felt accepted when the kids asked me to play ball with them."

DIALOGUE:

See that boy who's new on the team. He feels accepted because they want him to bat next. I remember feeling accepted when . . .

Can you think of a time when you felt accepted?

I bet you felt real good about yourself.

Did you feel like you belonged in the group?

So now we know what that feeling is when we feel accepted.

What other feelings can you think of that start with the letter A?

This blank page is for you to draw or write how you felt when you were feeling brave.

B **is for feeling BRAVE**

"I'm going to be brave this time and slide down the high slide."

DIALOGUE:

See this little girl. She's feeling brave about sliding down the high slide.
I remember feeling brave when . . .

Can you think of a time when you felt brave?

I bet you felt proud of yourself then, didn't you?

Did you feel, right then, that you could handle anything?

So now we know what that feeling is when we feel brave.

What other feelings can you think of that start with the letter B?

This blank page is for you to draw or write how you felt when you were feeling confused.

C *is for feeling CONFUSED*

"Tommy invited me to come and see his new puppy, and Susie's cat just had kittens. I don't know where to go first. I feel confused."

DIALOGUE:

See that boy. He feels confused because he's having a hard time choosing where to go. I remember feeling confused when . . .

Can you think of a time when you felt confused?

When a person feels confused, it's a good idea to stop what he's doing, take a few deep breaths, and relax inside. That helps him choose what he wants most.

So now we know what that feeling is when we feel confused.

What other feelings can you think of that start with the letter C?

This blank page is for you to draw or write how you felt when you were feeling disappointed.

D is for feeling DISAPPOINTED

"Bingo got to eat my ice cream instead of me. I'm so disappointed."

DIALOGUE:

See that girl who just lost her ice cream. She's feeling disappointed because she wanted to eat it, and now her dog is lapping it up. Once when I felt disappointed . . .

Can you think of a time when you felt disappointed?

We feel disappointed when something we want to happen doesn't happen, or when we don't get what we want.

When you felt disappointed, did you feel tired, and just wanted to go where no one would see you?

So now we know what that feeling is when we feel disappointed.

What other feelings can you think of that start with the letter D?

This blank page is for you to draw or write how you felt when you were feeling excited.

E *is for feeling EXCITED*

"I feel excited because it's my birthday."

DIALOGUE:

See that birthday boy. He's feeling excited because he's celebrating his special day with his friends. I remember feeling excited when . . .

Can you think of a time when you felt excited?

It sounds like you were really happy, knowing good things were about to happen. I bet you felt like a rocket ready to take off.

So now we know what that feeling is when we feel excited.

What other feelings can you think of that start with the letter E?

This blank page is for you to draw or write how you felt when you were feeling friendly.

is for feeling FRIENDLY

"I feel friendly when I say 'Hi' to our mail carrier."

DIALOGUE:

See that girl saying "Hi" to the mail carrier. The little girl feels friendly because she sees someone she likes. Once when I felt friendly . . .

Can you think of a time when you felt friendly?

I guess feeling friendly is when you like to meet new people and see old friends, too. It makes you feel happy inside, doesn't it?

So now we know what that feeling is when we feel friendly.

What other feelings can you think of that start with the letter F?

This blank page is for you to draw or write how you felt when you were feeling generous.

is for feeling GENEROUS

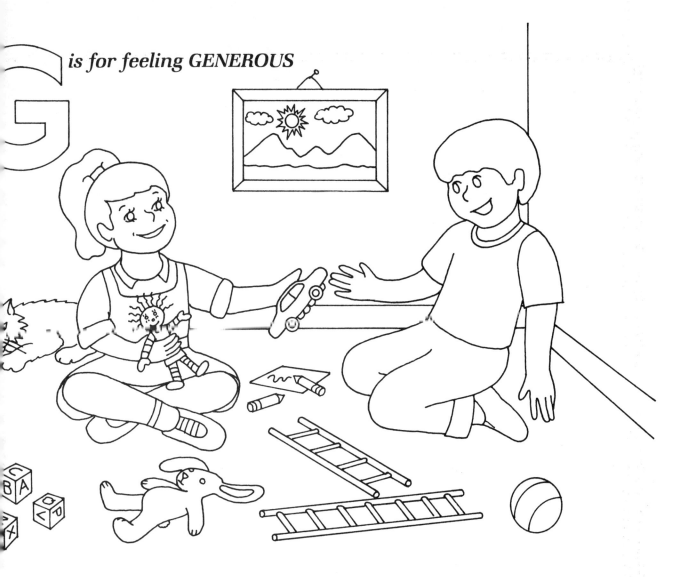

"I feel generous when I share my toys."

LOGUE:

*that little girl giving her toy to her friend. She feels generous when
s able to give something special. I remember feeling generous
n . . .*

you think of a time when you felt generous?

*t you felt you were sharing something that was special to you. Did
feel, right then, that your heart was super-big?*

ow we know what that feeling is when we feel generous.

t other feelings can you think of that start with the letter G?

This blank page is for you to draw or write how you felt when you were feeling helpful.

H is for feeling HELPFUL

"I feel helpful when I'm cooking with my mother."

DIALOGUE:

See that boy is feeling helpful by stirring what he and his mother are cooking. I remember feeling helpful . . .

Can you think of a time when you felt helpful?

You must have felt you made it easier by doing what you could do. And you liked yourself for doing what you did.

So now we know what that feeling is when we feel helpful.

What other feelings can you think of that start with the letter H?

This blank page is for you to draw or write how you felt when you we
feeling important.

I is for feeling IMPORTANT

"I feel important when Daddy asks me to work with him in the garden."

DIALOGUE:

See that child planting in the garden with her father. She feels important working side-by-side with her Daddy. I remember feeling important when . . .

Can you think of a time when you felt important?

I bet you felt you did something wonderful. Sounds like someone knows you can do wonderful things.

So now we know what that feeling is when we feel important.

What other feelings can you think of that start with the letter I?

This blank page is for you to draw or write how you felt when you wer feeling jealous.

J is for feeling JEALOUS

"I feel jealous of his new scooter."

DIALOGUE:

See that boy with the old scooter. He feels jealous because his friend has a brand new one. I remember feeling jealous . . .

Can you think of a time when you felt jealous?

Did you feel it wasn't fair, because he has what you wanted?

Sounds like you wanted to change places with someone else.

So now we know what that feeling is when we feel jealous.

What other feelings can you think of that start with the letter J?

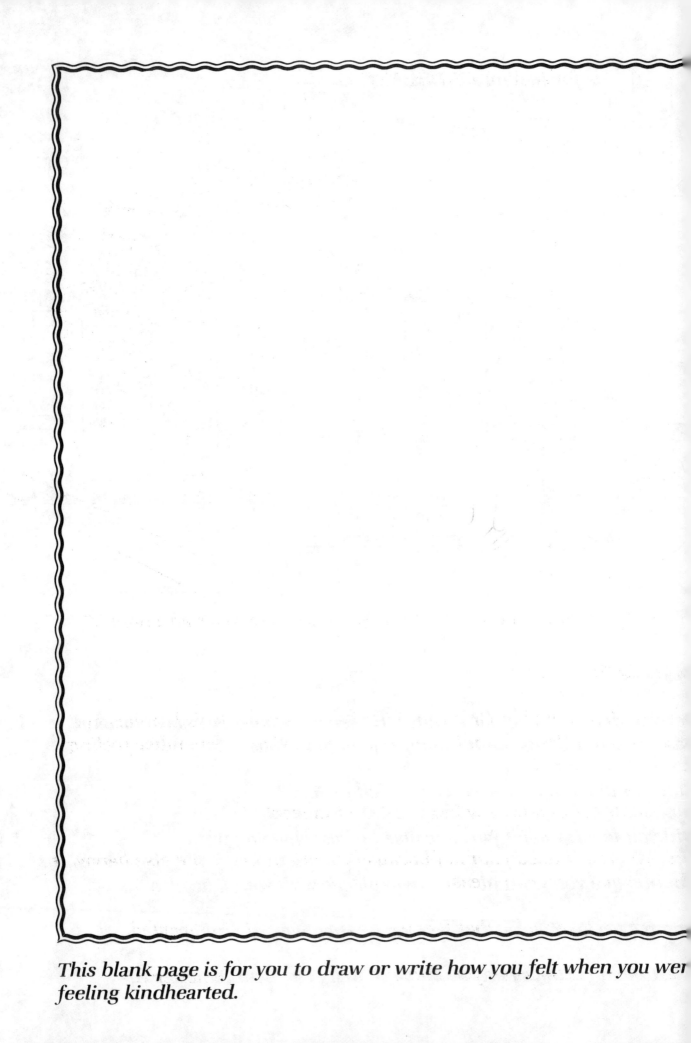

This blank page is for you to draw or write how you felt when you wer[e]
feeling kindhearted.

K *is for feeling KINDHEARTED*

"I feel kindhearted when I take Grandpa his glasses and paper."

DIALOGUE:

See the girl taking her Grandpa what he needs. She feels kindhearted because she's doing something for someone else. I remember feeling kindhearted when . . .

Can you think of a time when you felt kindhearted?

I bet you really liked yourself because you made someone else happy. It pleases you when you please someone else, doesn't it?

So now we know what that feeling is when we feel kindhearted.

What other feelings can you think of that start with the letter K?

This blank page is for you to draw or write how you felt when you were feeling loving.

is for feeling LOVING

"I love my turtle just the way he is."

DIALOGUE:

See that child petting his turtle, because he feels loving towards it.
Once when I felt loving . . .

Can you think of a time when you felt loving?

Sounds like you felt warm and full of goodness, like everything was
wonderful in your world.

So now we know what that feeling is when we feel loving.

What other feelings can you think of that start with the letter L?

This blank page is for you to draw or write how you felt when you wer[e]
feeling mad.

M is for feeling MAD

"I'm mad at you right now. You better leave me alone, you bully."

DIALOGUE:

See the boy with rollerblades. He feels mad because that bigger boy purposely tripped him. Once when I felt mad...

Can you think of a time when you felt mad?

It sounds like you wanted to scream at someone, because you felt so angry.

So now we know what that feeling is when we feel mad.

What other feelings can you think of that start with the letter M?

This blank page is for you to draw or write how you felt when you were feeling naughty.

N is for feeling NAUGHTY

"I'm feeling naughty because my sister is looking for her homework, and I hid it. I just wanted to play a joke on her, but she says I'm naughty."

DIALOGUE:

See that little girl who hid her big sister's papers. She's feeling naughty for what she's done. Once when I felt naughty . . .

Can you think of a time when you felt naughty?

Do you think you did it just because you wanted to be naughty? I bet you felt like you did something you shouldn't have done, and you could have been in big trouble for doing it.

So now we know what that feeling is when we feel naughty.

What other feelings can you think of that start with the letter N?

This blank page is for you to draw or write how you felt when you were feeling O.K.

is for feeling O.K.

"When I'm feeling O.K., I'm feeling somewhere between terrific and not-so-terrific, but that's O.K."

DIALOGUE:

See the face in the middle. That's how a person feels when he feels O.K. He doesn't feel happy and he doesn't feel unhappy. He just feels O.K. Once when I felt O.K. . . .

Can you think of a time when you felt O.K.?

It's not high or low; it's in the middle — feeling comfortable with yourself.

So now we know what that feeling is when we feel O.K.

What other feelings can you think of that start with the letter O?

This blank page is for you to draw or write how you felt when you were feeling peaceful.

P *is for feeling PEACEFUL*

"When I hear a bedtime story in front of the fireplace, I feel peaceful."

DIALOGUE:

See that child on his father's lap. He feels peaceful, listening to a bedtime story, told by his Daddy. Once when I felt peaceful . . .

Can you think of a time when you felt peaceful?

I bet you felt content, like there were no problems to think about. When we're peaceful, things seem so calm and quiet that we can even hear ourselves breathing.

So now we know what that feeling is when we feel peaceful.

What other feelings can you think of that start with the letter P?

This blank page is for you to draw or write how you felt when you were feeling quizzical.

is for feeling QUIZZICAL

"I feel quizzical when I ask a lot of questions."

DIALOGUE:

See that child on top of the clothes dryer. She feels quizzical, because she wants to know all about how the dryer works. Once when I felt quizzical . . .

Can you think of a time when you felt quizzical?

Sounds like you were curious, like the little girl in the picture. You wanted to know the answers to your questions.

So now we know what that feeling is when we feel quizzical.

What other feelings can you think of that start with the letter Q?

This blank page is for you to draw or write how you felt when you were feeling responsible.

R *is for feeling RESPONSIBLE*

"I feel responsible when I do my job of feeding the fish."

DIALOGUE:

See that boy feeding the fish. He feels responsible because he's in charge of seeing to it that the fish eat every day. Once when I felt responsible . . .

Can you think of a time when you felt responsible?

It makes you feel all grown-up, doesn't it? Like you have a job just like people who go to work.

So now we know what that feeling is when we feel responsible.

What other feelings can you think of that start with the letter R?

This blank page is for you to draw or write how you felt when you were feeling sad.

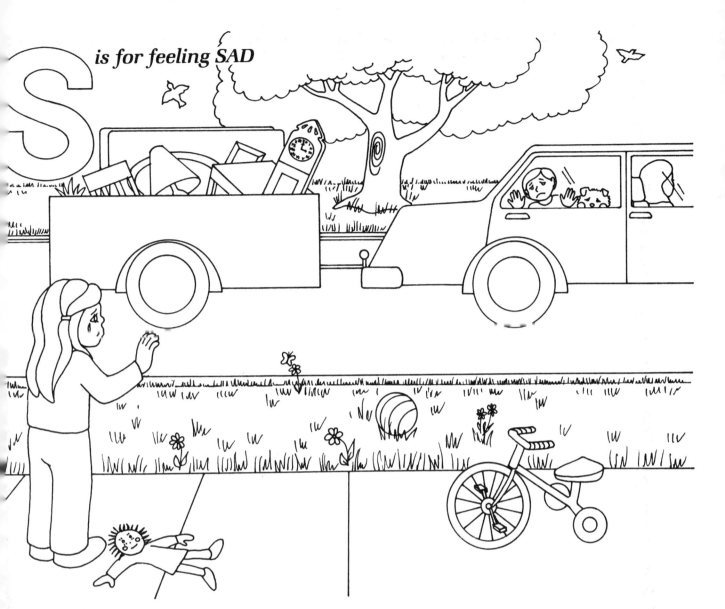

is for feeling SAD

"I'm sad because my friend is moving away."

DIALOGUE:

See that girl waving goodbye to the boy in the car. She feels sad because he's going to live in another town. Once when I felt sad . . .

Can you think of a time when you felt sad?

I bet you felt like crying. Maybe you did cry — that's what many people do when they're unhappy or sad.

So now we know what that feeling is when we feel sad.

What other feelings can you think of that start with the letter S?

This blank page is for you to draw or write how you felt when you were feeling thankful.

T is for feeling THANKFUL

"I feel thankful for my family."

DIALOGUE:

See that family bowing their heads and folding their hands. They feel thankful for their food and for being together. Once when I felt thankful . . .

Can you think of a time when you felt thankful?

Sounds like you were grateful for what you had. You just wanted to say, "Thank you, thank you, thank you!"

So now we know what that feeling is when we feel thankful.

What other feelings can you think of that start with the letter T?

This blank page is for you to draw or write how you felt when you were feeling unique.

U is for feeling UNIQUE

"No one else in the whole world has my fingerprint. I feel unique."

DIALOGUE:

See the child's thumb black with ink. He put his thumbprint on the paper, and now he knows how unique he is. I especially felt unique when . . .

Can you tell me one way you know you are unique?

I bet you feel like you are one-of-a-kind, a super-special child.

So now we know what that feeling is when we feel unique.

What other feelings can you think of that start with the letter U?

This blank page is for you to draw or write how you felt when you were feeling victorious.

V is for feeling VICTORIOUS

"I felt victorious when I was one of the winners in the Read-A-Thon contest at school."

DIALOGUE:

See those three children, holding their certificates of winning. They all feel victorious. Once when I felt victorious . . .

Can you think of a time when you felt victorious?

Seems like your hard work paid off. You felt victorious because you reached your goal and wanted everyone to know it.

So now we know what that feeling is when we feel victorious.

What other feelings can you think of that start with the letter V?

This blank page is for you to draw or write how you felt when you were feeling worried.

W *is for feeling WORRIED*

"I'm worried I'll be late for school."

DIALOGUE:

See that little girl waiting for her mother to take her to school. The little girl feels worried because she doesn't want to be late. Once when I felt worried . . .

Can you think of a time when you felt worried?

I bet you felt you couldn't stop thinking about that one thing. It just wouldn't go out of your mind until it was taken care of.

So now we know what that feeling is when we feel worried.

What other feelings can you think of that start with the letter W?

This blank page is for you to draw or write how you felt when you were feeling exhausted.

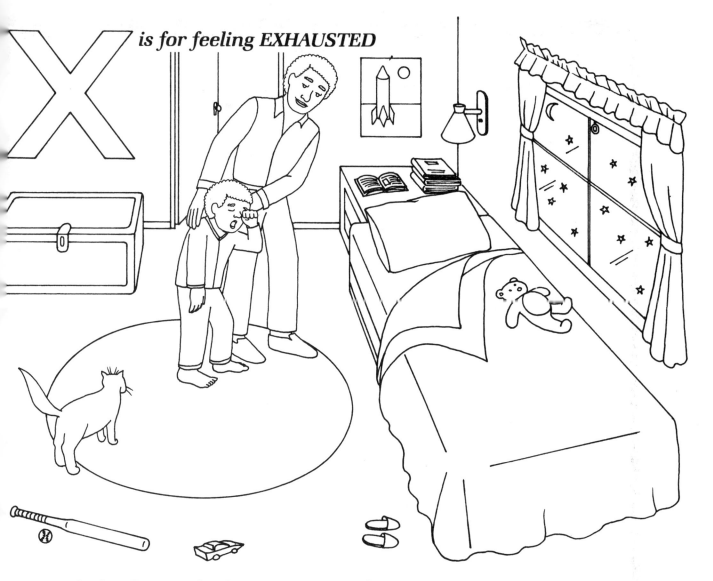

X *is for feeling EXHAUSTED*

"I feel exhausted when I'm so tired I just want to go to sleep."

DIALOGUE:

See that boy. He can hardly walk into his bedroom, because he feels so exhausted. Once when I felt exhausted . . .

Can you think of a time when you felt exhausted?

Sounds like your body felt so heavy you could barely move it. You didn't want to talk or do anything.

So now we know what that feeling is when we feel exhausted.

What other feelings can you think of that start with the letter X?

This blank page is for you to draw or write how you felt when you wer[e]
feeling yucky.

Y *is for feeling YUCKY.*

"Cleaning up raw eggs on the floor makes me feel yucky."

DIALOGUE:

See that girl wiping up the broken eggs. It feels yucky to her when she touches raw eggs. Once I felt yucky when . . .

Can you think of a time when you felt yucky?

I bet you felt like you didn't want anyone to touch you. Sometimes when people are sick, they feel yucky, and just want to be alone.

So now we know what that feeling is when we feel yucky.

What other feelings can you think of that start with the letter Y?

This blank page is for you to draw or write how you felt when you wer
feeling zippy.

Z *is for feeling ZIPPY*

"When I feel zippy, I feel full of energy."

DIALOGUE:

See that little boy smiling and jumping in the sunshine. He feels zippy because he can be outside, and do a lot of things. Once when I felt zippy . . .

Can you think of a time when you felt zippy?

Seems like you felt you could go as high as the sky, like everything was going great for you.

So now we know what that feeling is when we feel zippy.

What other feelings can you think of that start with the letter Z?

Unique Products for Children <u>and</u> Adults

LEARNING/COLORING BOOK

A unique 64 page 8 1/2" x 11" book offering guidance in communication of feelings correlating with the alphabet. Each letter has a dialogue to explore the feelings associated with that letter, as well as a black and white illustration which can be used for coloring. Includes a Curriculum/Activity Guide printed inside.
Recommended by ALA Booklist.

60 MINUTE COMPANION AUDIO TAPE

A fun adventure into music and sound for children of all ages to explore 26 different feelings. Music and sounds by Bob Mills. Features songs: "I Still Love You", "I'm Sad Today", "The Zippy Song".
Recommended by ALA Booklist.

FEELINGS AWARENESS CHART

(8 1/2" x 11") A laminated chart with 354 different feelings to discover while increasing vocabulary! Great to use with the ABC Feelings Learning Book.

FEELINGS POSTCARD

A miniature version of the color poster.

COMBO PACKAGES:
(Shrink-Wrapped)

- *Learning/Coloring Book & Audio Tape.*
- *Book, Tape & Feelings Awareness Chart.*
- *Book, Tape, Folded Poster & FREE Postcard.*

MULTICULTURAL POSTER

22" x 28". Ideal for home, office or classroom. Each of the 26 colorful drawings denotes a feeling associated with that letter.

Feelings Awareness Activity Kit 1

- ➤ *64 Page Learning/Coloring Book*
- ➤ *60 Minute Audio Tape*
- ➤ *35 Coloring Place Mats*
- ➤ *22" x 28" Color Poster (folded)*
- ➤ *Laminated Feelings Awareness Chart*
- ➤ *Full Color Lotto/Bingo Game*

INCLUDES <u>FREE</u> "HOW TO" CURRICULUM/ACTIVITY GUIDE!

Feelings Awareness Activity Kit 2

- ➤ *64 Page Learning/Coloring Book*
- ➤ *60 Minute Audio Tape*
- ➤ *Laminated Coloring Place Mat*
- ➤ *22" x 28" Color Poster (folded)*
- ➤ *Feelings Awareness Chart*
- ➤ *Full Color Lotto/Bingo Game*

INCLUDES <u>FREE</u> "HOW TO" CURRICULUM/ACTIVITY GUIDE!

COTTON T-SHIRTS

Screen printed on white 100% cotton. Features the ABC Feelings graphics in full color. Available in the following sizes:

Child/Youth: *Small (6-8), Medium (10-12) and Large (14-16)*
Adult: *Small, Medium, Large, X Large and XX Large*

PLACE MAT/MINI POSTER

11" x 17" with laminated "wipe clean" surface. Same colorful drawings as the full size poster. Reverse side blank for child to draw how he/she feels. Also a wall decoration.

FLOOR PUZZLE

This 23" x 37" 30-piece puzzle is a large version of the color mini poster. Children will love fitting together the pieces while learning about feelings and the ABCs.

COLORING PLACE MATS

(11" x 17") Ideal for home or classroom. Children learn about feelings while coloring creatively. (35 per pkg)

LOTTO GAME

A fun learning game for 2 to 7 players using all the colorful ABC Feelings characters.

FEELINGS AWARENESS ACTIVITY/FLASH CARDS

(7 1/2" x 8 3/4") 26 cards per set with full color illustrations and a feeling word for each letter. Each card has a line drawing on the back, a definition of the feeling, a story and interesting activities relating to that feeling. 6 activities per card for preschool age and up. Perfect for home or classroom, group or one on one. Instructions included. Packaged for handy use and carrying.

We hope you enjoyed your ABC FEELINGS book. We invite you to order the other exciting ABC FEELINGS products and additional copies of the book for friends - they make great gifts!

ABC FEELINGS products are available at stores throughout the USA, as well as several other countries. If you are unable to find them at a nearby store, please write or call:

ABC FEELINGS, INC.

Formerly Adage Publications

P.O. Box 2377, Coeur d'Alene, ID 83816-2377   (208) 762-3177
e-mail: feelings@iea.com

CLOSING

Now that you've learned your ABC's and can recognize 26 different feelings you have, you can express them wisely and know it's O.K. Expressing your feelings is expressing your honesty. You'll be healthier and happier, and feel good about yourself and your life. It's the only way to go.